The *Beauty* in the Broken

A. Bova

Copyright © 2020 by A.B.Baird Publishing

All rights reserved. This book or any portion thereof may not be reproduced or used in any manner whatsoever without the express written permission of the publisher except for the use of brief quotations in a book review.

Printed in the United States of America

First Printing, 2020

ISBN 978-1-949321-18-0

All writings within this book belong to the author.

Cover Art Image by: Shari Ryan

A.B.Baird Publishing

66548 Highway 203

La Grande OR, 97850

USA

www.abbairdpublishing.com

To the lighthouse keepers, the lovers, the fighters, the dreamers, the stargazers—the hopeful hearts that have scraped their knees—this one is for you. I love you. You are enough.

Always.

Table of Contents

Unraveling	9-53
Stained Glass	10
Empath Song	11
Tired Bones	12
Worthless	13
Sober	14
Kindling	15
Fast Food	16
Spill	17
Unraveling	18
Trick Candles	19
Shatter	20
Anchor	21
Soul Catching	22
Confessions	23
Wednesday	24
Some Sum	25
Connect the Dots	26
Sweater Weather	27
Lock & Key	28
Speak	29
To Pray Against	30

Battered Cages	31
Secondhand I Love You	32
Home is Where the Heart Is	33
Haunted House	34
Dark Corners	35
Monster	36
Maroon	37
Shadows	38
Carry the Darkness	39
Panic	40
Silent Girl	41
Suffocate	42
Weary	43
Storm Chaser	44
Puddle Jumper	45
Goodbye Kiss	46
Bargain Hunters	47
Bottled Up	48
Poetry Lines	49
Catch-22	50
Heads Up	51
The Sculptor	52
Love Letter	53

Reprieve (a breath)	55-71
Infectious Sky	56
Hey Lovely	57
Heart to Hearts	58
Love Stays Down	59
Carry On	60
Home Improvement	61
Catch Me	62
Clean Slate	63
Barter	64
Sun Up	65
Watermelon Seed	66
Hide	67
Wildflower Love	68
Dear Lover	69
Heartbeat Sound	70
Read in Between the Lines	71
Becoming	73-115
Morning Mirror	74
Reflection	75
Bruise	76
Winter Girl	77
Worthy	78

Skipping Stones	79
Eyes Closed	80
Wreckage	81
Memory Lane	82
Fluttering Ghosts	83
Dance Dance	84
Forest Fires	85
Bury	86
If You're Reading This	87
Forgiveness Garden	88
Growing Pains	89
Rise	90
The Head & The Heart	91
Interrogation	92
Father Time	93
Paper Cranes	94
Crushed	95
Get Well Soon	96
Love on Your Arms	97
Survival	98
Never Enough	99
Soul Sister	100-101
Graveyards	102
Thank You	103

Forked Road	104
Postcard	105
Love Me	106
Exhale	107
Fog	108
Remarkable Things	109
Hyacinths	110
Our Story	111
I Left a Piece of You in Every Poem	112-113
Finish Line	114
Lady Lazarus	115
Acknowledgments:	116

Unraveling

...

A. Bova

Stained Glass

I know you feel broken.
I will sit with you
and your broken pieces
and make a stained glass window

Empath Song

I absorb others' emotions like a sponge
elbows deep in dirt
from other people's gardens
with my watering can heart.

I am tired
        but hopeful

Hopeful for the flowers drinking my empath song

A. Bova

Tired Bones

I stitch your tired bones
together with the best intentions
two hundred and six
        chances
                to build you up...

Worthless

You tell me I'm as worthless
as wearing a raincoat as protection
against the waves.

When the bad days stay,
I'm soaked to the bone,
        wringing out salt water from my hair
        and hope from my heart

Sober

Sober words hit the hardest
because I knew you couldn't
shove blame into my pocket
                    and save it for later

Kindling

You have used
the pages of my story
as kindling for a fire
that I have never gotten
to warm my hands on

Fast Food

She made it further than the fast—
eating only the words you left under her pillow,

rationing out affection
too sweet against her teeth
and hurt
too hard to swallow
without a glass of water
to keep it down

Spill

Bite your tongue, darling.
Blood is pooling against
        your quivering lips,
              waiting to spill the truth

Unraveling

Unravel the fabric of my soul,
pinch me at the seams.
I hope you construct
the person you want
in the end

Trick Candles

My path was lit
by trick candles—
relighting themselves
every time the air
escaped my lungs,
my knees rising
to my chest to fill up
where my breath has gone
as I watch the sparklers
reignite and dance
beside themselves—
a delusion embracing

A. Bova

Shatter

You shattered my soul
the day my uncle left this earth.
I begged,
          and begged,
                        and begged

for you to do it on another day—any day

—BROKEN—

at a funeral.
I could not figure out
who the tears were for

Anchor

Your smile is weighed down by loss,
      an anchor,
           pulling at the edges of your mouth,
                down,
                down,

                down to where the darkness lives

Soul Catching

And then there were none—
no soul catching clavicle kisses,
no ear whispering,
no pounding chest,
          loving hearts
to scoop up
      and mend
              over Friday morning coffee

Confessions

My nightstand drawers are full of apologies,
                crumpled up confessions
                      crossed out
                      in black ink

A. Bova

Wednesday

Forget my name—
it's a lost item
      never found,
left on a park bench
      on a rainy Wednesday

Some Sum

Some arms weren't meant for holding—
some hands weren't meant for love.
And some words weren't meant for poetry,
but I've pulled them from my mouth like teeth
                                      to extract the past

A. Bova

Connect the Dots

There are constellations mapped across my back,

a pale pink sky
covered with beauty mark stars
you used to connect with your fingertips.

Spelling out the truth with your hands

Sweater Weather

I was wearing my favorite sweater
               the day I realized
                         you weren't coming back,
my fingers tucked in the sleeves,
               pulling at a loose thread—
                       hope on a string...

A. Bova

Lock & Key

My body has held her own screams
under lock and key.
I have choked
on my own silence—
wondering
where all the dead words have gone

Speak

My mother tongue never
translated to a *love language*

A. Bova

To Pray Against

Self-deprecation:
pressed like flowers
between old dictionary pages

Battered Cages

Our skeletons are made
of scattered lines of p o e t r y
the fingers loose with longing,
grasping at other people's hearts
inside their battered cages,
begging to be read

A. Bova

Secondhand I Love You

You deserve more than a secondhand *I love you*

You deserve more than a cracked spine,
worn-out cover kind of love

Home Is Where the Heart Is

You left the door open
so anyone could come in
no longer worried where
I laid my head at night
or whose eyes or hands
painted every inch
of who you used to call home

A. Bova

Haunted House

My thoughts
take the dusty white sheets off the furniture
and wear them as armor against the darkness—
ghosts wandering the halls of this house
haunted by the remains
of happy days

Dark Corners

I have been hiding
in the dark corners,
abandoning breaths

A. Bova

Monster

I've been afraid
of what lives in the darkness,
depression, a shadow
that hides in the corner
of my bedroom,

the monster that grabs my ankle

as soon as sleep
      wraps its heavy arms
            around my shoulders.

Keep the light on for me—
      my eyes wide open

Maroon

A maroon-hearted girl and her demons
dance together in the shadows,
a flashlight painting
their silhouette across the walls she built

brick
by
brick...

A. Bova

Shadows

She gathers up her shadows in her arms
straight off the floor,
creasing the corners,
and folding them into
gentle piles
to wear another day

Carry the Darkness

I rock loneliness
in my arms, cradling
and carrying the darkness in my hands
until it is sound asleep

A. Bova

Panic

Panic is the only thing
that kisses me good morning,
      my eyelids crackling awake
      to the palpitations
      playing against the cage

Silent Girl

Anxiety crawls up my throat
to steal my voice again

I am a girl left mute
on the edge of her mind

A. Bova

Suffocate

I suffocate under the weight
of an anxious mind,
letting the air
out of my helium balloon lungs,
deflated promises
left on my lips when
         alone is the last place I'd rather be

Weary

My soul is tired—
forehead pressed against the bus window,
searching the city lights
for fragments of you
to rest my weary eyes on

A. Bova

Storm Chaser

I used to love the sound of thunderstorms—
the low rumble and cracks against the black—
breaking the sky into tiny pieces of night.
I compared my pieces with the sky,
lying flat on my back
against the damp grass to compare scars.

We look alike, I begged.
Then I felt the rain come

Puddle Jumper

I am a puddle jumper
even with depression rising to my knees.
It's so hard to dance when the storm comes.
I wear my heart
       in my rain boots—
              always afraid of getting wet

A. Bova

Goodbye Kiss

The fog misses you,
pulling you back in.
Another. Then another.
The light looks hazy in the distance,
and he turns your face back to his,
distracting you with the comfort
                      of a not-so-lonely bed

Bargain Hunters

Depression is in the business of misery,
and we bargain with days by the handful,
a debt that is never paid

Bottled Up

I keep my feelings
bottled up
so I can sell them on the black market—
      some overpriced empathy,
      and pure guilt
      bitter on the tongue.

I've traded them
for an awful lot of things,
      buyer's remorse sitting
      heavy
      where you used to be

Poetry Lines

Depression feeds me
poetry lines
      dangling grapes
      above my mouth,
           coaxing them out of me...

Catch-22

Rest your mind
like you rest your eyes
closed, with the blinds shut.

What is worse than tired?

I have accepted
that mental illness
is the Catch-22 of my life.
Avenues of recovery
often look like Rorschach tests—
an algorithm with a lot of pretty colors
and no right answer.

Heads-Up

Sometimes, I flip a quarter in my palm to cheat chance.
I always pick *heads*.
Heads always seemed
like the positive answer
like tails were the afterthought,
the 'left' when people say 'right'—
Did that make it wrong?
I am the unluckiest person
I have ever met, but still
I try to bring karma into my circle.

Sometimes, that quarter does read
heads, but I feel like it's more
of a message, like,
*"Just wanted to give you a heads-up
that something bad will happen today,"*
or
*"Keep your hopes up high,
and your head down low,"*
like that *A Day to Remember* song
you memorized in college.

I cannot keep my hopes up
and keep my head down
and pretend like the universe
doesn't give me signs I cannot read.

*Maybe I should stop carrying around change
like it will bring some my way*

A. Bova

The Sculptor

I have been chiseling away at the pretty parts of me,
wondering if I can sculpt
a masterpiece
like those long-gone artists
who were confident in their definition
of what beauty could be

Love Letter

The love letters we write to ourselves
are never written in pen,
eraser at the ready

A. Bova

Reprieve
(a breath)

...

A. Bova

Infectious Sky

We were like the moon and the sun that way—
lovers never fated to stay in one place,
always chasing,
we meet in an infectious sky—
a star for every kiss
you left against me

Hey, Lovely

I never know what to do with my face
when someone compliments me.
I thought about what I would say to myself
if I could date me,
unlike the brutal one-liners
I've received with angst
"Hey, baby, what's your sign?"
"I'm a Leo," I want to say,
but I act more like a Cancer,
and, also, I couldn't give a shit about astrology,
but I would love to post a 'Stop' sign
across my chest
as a greeting.

I've learned
it's better to keep your mouth shut
than spill your guts
to the people
who will always
take advantage of your kindness.
Take advantage of the length of your skirt.

Take advantage of *you*.

Heart to Hearts

"How is the stuff between your ears
and behind your ribs?" he asked.
My mother always told me that
if I didn't have anything nice to say,
I shouldn't say it at all.
I want to tell him my heart beats
in my teeth most days—
that I itch *because I want
to come out of my skin.*
My soul cannot stretch wide enough
against rib cage walls.

Don't try to put me back in.

Maybe I could tell him
in these heart to hearts—
they could sit beside one another,
shoulders grazing, and get down,
all the way down to where the secrets are buried—

>   Beat twice if you're okay.
>   Beat twice if you're only trying
>   your very best to stay alive

Love Stays Down

Do jumping jacks when you're upset, he said.
It gets your heart rate up, he said.

Yet my body is so tired of flailing—
leaping into things
with my arms pinned to my sides
so the love stays down

Carry On

Don't you dare fall in love with me.
A cardboard box full of problems
will end up on your doorstep
      full of big sweaters,
      depression,
      coffee,

      and one long lost hair tie.

Sometimes I forget about my things
when I share them with you.

Then I remember
that the weight
of my world
      is easier to carry

      alone

Home Improvement

You can't build a home in me, I say.
My hands are unscathed—unworn.
When you pull apart the walls,
you will find everything that cannot be fixed.
Get rid of me.
Leave the rotting wood and wallpaper to me

A. Bova

Catch Me

Catch me if you can—
the wind whistling through your fingers,
grabbing fistfuls of air
to whisper secrets to

Clean Slate

Keep me warm
when the darkness sets in—
cold and damp, resting in my bones
I cannot be wiped clean.
Press your body right up against my soul

> *where it hurts to breathe*

A. Bova

Barter

I barter with lipstick stained coffee mugs
filled with whiskey
left alone in the sink
after 3 a.m. kisses

Sun Up

Insomniac dreamers promise each other the world
when the morning first kisses the sky—
a blush rising in her cheeks

A. Bova

Watermelon Seed

Our love was the size of a watermelon seed—
you swallowed it down,
and you were convinced you would die,
but really, we were watching love grow
                              grow
                              grow...

Hide

Your smirk stayed tucked
in my collarbone,
and I kept it there
just in case
        you ever needed
               a place to hide

A. Bova

Wildflower Love

Roses used to bloom at our feet.
Now we have a wildflower love
that people mistake for weeds,

and we carry them

pressed against our chests
so we never lose the scent.

I weave them in my hair *like promises*

The Beauty in the Broken

Dear Lover

The closest thing I've ever gotten to perfect was you.
I could spend the rest of my days drinking
from your fountain of youth *and never grow old.*

Your laugh is the kind of thing
they sell on the black market for a pretty penny,
but you've gifted me with this joy for free.

I am spoiled rotten
by the way your weighted-blanket arms
wrap around me every night,
telling the darkness to take a hike.

The darkness doesn't always listen.
But your soul is an open door
that I've spent a lot of time slamming,
and still, you've given me a key—
a key I keep around my neck
that presses against our heartbeat sound.

Your mouth is the prettiest place
I have ever been,
and I keep postcards I've drawn from memory.

I've never claimed to be an artist,
but you have them pinned to your fridge
for safe keeping

A. Bova

Heartbeat Sound

It is okay if this is your only constant—
that heartbeat sound against your ear,
the flowers drinking the warm rain,
the freckles sprinkled across your back like stars.
We can be the whole universe *if we try*

Read in Between the Lines

Read between the poetry lines—
find us pressed against the stanzas,
iambic pentameter crushed on our lips.
We are the spaces between words

A. Bova

Becoming

...

A. Bova

Morning Mirror

Can we fall in love
with the person who stares back
from the morning mirror—
the girl with bloodshot eyes,
cracked lips,
a worry crease
forever etched against
her laugh lines.

We balance
on the edge of forgiveness

Reflection

I'm killing myself to stay alive today

the girl in the mirror
doesn't look like a person I remember,
but I press my palms against the reflection
and ask for her forgiveness anyway
for all the times I cursed her name
for all the times I pinched
her caterpillar elbow scar
for all the times I told her
I didn't love her
for all the times I thought she didn't deserve
to own the word "beauty"
and wear it like a new dress

I ask for her forgiveness
for all the times before

A. Bova

Bruise

Pain has kissed my pale skin
with black and blue.
Everything will darken
before it heals.
We bruise,
and we get better

Winter Girl

Tell your mental health
she looks beautiful
in that dress she is wearing—
that her winter freckles
are the perfect shade of pink
against her chapped skin

A. Bova

Worthy

Do not leave your soul on empty.

You give love to everyone but yourself.

Who needs it more?

Who deserves to be lifted from the ashes every evening and brush off the dust?

Who is more worthy than you?

Skipping Stones

You've given away
the very best parts of you—
and they feel like
smooth skipping stones
weighing down forgotten palms.
If only they would
>	*just*
>	*hold*
>	*on*

A. Bova

Eyes Closed

Marlboro Special Blends
stain every inch of my memory—
the ones I can trace
with my eyes closed.
I steal cigarettes from
strangers' mouths
to remember the taste of you

Wreckage

There were beautiful moments
among all that wreckage

Memory Lane

Every time I walk down memory lane,
I forget my umbrella at home—
on the streets dressed in maple trees
and forgotten things

Fluttering Ghosts

Our memories come to me like forehead kisses—
    light, fluttering ghosts
    disguised as love

A. Bova

Dance Dance

Let's dance to the sound
our memories make
as they leave us

Forest Fires

To think I miss our forest fires—
the way they would ignite
with just a hint of a spark.
I felt loved when you would fight with me—
jealousy, like whiskey on your breath.
Our noses would meet in protest—
the glare, sitting on the edge of your eyes,
daring me to challenge you—
to challenge love as I knew it.
Our slice of paradise looked an awful lot like hell,

and we loved watching it burn

Bury

Sometimes healing
looks a lot like burying
a beating heart.

You can always grow flowers
where the dirt used to be

If You're Reading This

...I'm sorry.

I carried around the remains of us
for longer than I meant to.
Sometimes pain
is begging to be free

A. Bova

Forgiveness Garden

When you plant seeds,
sometimes you don't know
what will bloom
when the spring comes.

I start a forgiveness garden
        in the back-corner plot of my mind,
                      fingernails caked in dirt—
my head bowed in a silent prayer for rain in a drought
        that has made my mouth so dry
        I have forgotten
        what mercy tastes like against my lips

Growing Pains

Speak straight to my heart.
Ask her what she thinks survival looks like most days,
if growing pains are truly felt first at the toes,

if tears can really cleanse the soul

Rise

Wipe that pretty face, darling.
You thought you were done growing,
but the world had other plans.
You are not taller—but wiser.
Reach up to the heavens,
and thank it for the rain

The Head & The Heart

I always arrive late to the meeting
between my head and my heart

They are on different planets
yet in the same body—
seeing whose voice beats
the loudest against the cage,
whose voice I hear first when I enter,
coffee mug in hand

A. Bova

Interrogation

Have you ever sat down with your depression
in the interrogation room of your mind
and just asked, *"Why?"*

She was already read her Miranda rights,
but she doesn't need the warning to silence her.

Her handcuffs
glisten under the bright lights,
rubbing against her battered wrists.
Is there ever a motive—
sentencing for something that robs your sanity?

Is it still arson
if my brain is on fire
and no one was there to put it out?

Is it still kidnapping
if she has held my thoughts captive
against my will and confined me to loneliness?

Wrongful imprisonment.

The Beauty in the Broken

Father Time

I took a class on mental illness and meditation.
A girl in the circle asked the therapist
if they could take the clock off the wall
because she was afraid of time—
she was diagnosed with a terminal illness
that would never go away.
How could she ever be calm
when she was counting the ticks
leading up to a trial she never asked to be a part of?
Where the only verdict
would be the death penalty?
You go to class
to focus on the rhythm of your breath
and get reminded that life
can be shorter than an exhale.

It turns out, that clock was screwed into the wall
and couldn't come out.
I never saw the girl return to class.

Do not measure me with 525,600 minutes.
We will always be trying to beat Father Time
at a game no one asked to play

A. Bova

Paper Cranes

The universe
promises me a wish
if I construct 1,000 paper cranes,
but they crumble under the weight
of my clumsy thumbs—
my patience folded,
my forehead creased with worry.

And I wonder
what else my hands could make if given enough time

Crushed

The idea of giving up
sits like a crushed lightbulb
between my teeth

Get Well Soon

Do they have cards at Dollar Tree for mental health?

I scan the birthday cards,
    the anniversary cards,
        the sympathy cards
      that should be empathy cards

How do you say, *"Get well soon,"*
    knowing it won't be so soon?

I know I cannot put the wind back in your sails
with just one breath.
    I know locked jaws taste like static,
    so that's why I wrote it down.

Why can't the card read:
    "Hey, how is your depression?"
    "Hey, I just wanted to check on you,
    but I don't know what else to say,
    and I can't go and leave the inside
    of this card blank with no writing
    because then I spent 50 cents on failure
    when all I wanted to do
    was tell you that it's okay to not be okay
    for as long as you need to be."

Love On Your Arms

If you could write love on your arms,
what other words
would you etch across your skin?

Alive is a hard thing to be.

Every day is a chance
to stitch up the breaks
we make in our own hearts.

There is no never-ending story,
but the one you are writing
is full of magic

Survival

There is beauty
in scraping your knees
the tiny pebbles of gravel
stuck to your skin
like glitter gained
from surviving
rock bottom

Never Enough

Never enough, you say.
What a beautiful death it is
to be loved by you.
What an honor it was
to steal my name back
from your lips

Soul Sister

You thought I was bubbly
because I could be the one
with the secret stash of alcohol
at a college retreat in the mountains.

Turns out, I was just thrilled to be there.
Turns out, you had already chosen me.
Turns out, we are still doing this friendship thing.

Thank you.
You are the strongest thing
I have ever come across.
You punched life in the kneecap
with a crowbar—*the true story.*

The world has dealt you the worst hand,
and you have only ever received it with grace,
with a shot of Patron on the side.

I am proud of everything you are.
You are the woman
with the loudest baby dinosaur roar.
The woman with the best tea party menu.
The woman with the biggest Disney obsession.
The woman with the best heart.

The Beauty in the Broken

There will never be enough words
to explain how proud I am of you.
You have battled the darkest days
and still offer me an umbrella.
You have battled the darkest demons
and still offer to fight mine.

I will always be there
to drunk cry with you at sleepovers.
I will always help you pick up
the Jenga blocks of your life and reconstruct it
in the most beautiful and haphazard way.
My soul sister—
     you've got a friend in me.

Graveyards

I have stopped leaving my tired bones
in graveyards disguised as people

Thank You

Thank you, body,
for seeing this life thing through by my side.
You have learned how to breathe through the panic,
how to fight back against the dark,
how to remember that love
is not a journey you can take in a day.

Thank you, body,
for being patient with my mind—
her ways don't always make sense,
but she's just trying to survive,
to be a good partner to you.

You two never looked like soulmates,
but you have beaten the odds.

Forked Road

It is so hard to show people
scars that no one sees.

I try to stay fixated
on the forked road veins
kissing my wrists—

My pulse
the beat
to my road trip song,
carrying on

Postcard

Lifeline painted palms—
a postcard from all the places
my heart has gone without you

A. Bova

Love Me

The tide comes up to lick my toes,
a chill settling deeply
in the cracks between my bones

I think about that time
you said
no one would ever love me like you do

What a gift that is

Exhale

I have learned how to drown gracefully,
       arms outstretched, open—
       still against the darkness
       kissing down my spine.

Remind me what it's like to feel the exhale of peace

Fog

The fog will clear one morning

When you're frozen
on your couch
in your biggest blue cardigan
with the pockets that can fit
the entire world inside them.

You will be in the middle of sipping your coffee,
and it will taste a little bit like hope,
a flavor familiar but a little foreign.

You will welcome it,
praying there is room left
to hold it a little longer

Remarkable Things

If nobody speaks of remarkable things,
words will still hold dances
against my beating heart,

rattling the cage
until the sun peeks through my fingers

Hyacinths

Crushed hyacinths rest in the spine of our love story—
Forgiveness,
whispering against my fingertips

Our Story

I hope you find our story
on a used bookstore shelf,
and it still looks familiar—
dirty fingerprints pressed
against the pages—dog ears
caressing every corner

A. Bova

I Left a Piece of You in Every Poem

The poem I can't write
is addressed to you in **big bold letters**
      —italicized—
so you can pick it out easily in a lineup,
which is full of

Words. Haikus. Screams. Demands. Sadness.

A voice—crackling at the edges
that resembles something so familiar,
you swear you lived it.

And you did.
      With me.

A long time ago—
when love was just one of those windchime sounds
in the summertime.

When love seemed like a fruit
anyone could pick from the nearest tree.

When love looked a lot like each other,
even though the world told us otherwise.

I want you to know I have left a piece of you
in every poem I've ever written—

The Beauty in the Broken

    as a keepsake,
           a promise
                that Forever
sometimes lasts only a minute.

A day.   A month.   A year.   Four years.

That it could pass by faster
than you could blink your eyes.

And in my heart of hearts,
it has taken me this long to forgive you.
But I've finally taken off
this backpack of a burden I've been holding,
and I am setting it at your feet—
saying;
       "Thank you for your time."
       It's been a pleasure doing Love with you.

I know I will see you again,
pressed up against the book spine
in Barnes & Noble
in a town I've never been to.

I hope your fingertips smile
at this thing
we called
       Always.

Finish Line

I stay awake at night
hoping
that it's true—
maybe humanity
consists of the type of people
who hold hands while
crossing the finish line.

Run with me, darling.

Lady Lazarus

I'm that girl with Plath on her tongue,
a red-haired Lady Lazarus
dancing barefoot in her own poetic ashes

resurrecting

Acknowledgements:

This is for every family member and friend that helped me create this beauty—with listening ears and open hearts. Very few people will sit with you in the dark, and I am beyond lucky to have you.

To my parents—I have bottled up your endless love and support, and it has carried me through the darkest of days. Your love for each other and for your children are what dreams are made of. To my sisters—thank you for stalking my Instagram and supporting my passion. You have loved my words since the beginning of time. My first fans. Love love.

To my lighthouse keeper—you shine the brightest. Thank you for pushing me to be the best and cross the finish line on this collection. My world will forever be a better place with you in it. Keep shining, my friend.

To Esther Vivian Kay—for your support, love, and friendship from so far away. No words in English (or German!) could ever express my appreciation.

To A.B. Baird Publishing—thank you for giving my first poetry collection a home. This is a dream realized, and I can never thank you enough for providing a platform for so many writers.

To YOU—my reader—and for every heart and soul that has been shattered by this thing called life—may we all make our pain into stained glass windows.

www.ingramcontent.com/pod-product-compliance
Lightning Source LLC
LaVergne TN
LVHW041300080426
835510LV00009B/819